THE
AMAZING
MEMORY
BOOK

THE
AMAZING
MEMORY
BOOK

DOMINIC O'BRIEN

Thunder Bay
P · R · E · S · S

San Diego, California

Thunder Bay Press
An imprint of the Advantage Publishers Group
5880 Oberlin Drive, San Diego, CA 92121-4794
www.thunderbaybooks.com

Thunder Bay Edition 2005

All notations of errors or omissions should be addressed to Thunder
Bay Press, Editorial Department, at the above address. All other cor-
respondence (author inquiries, permissions) concerning the content
of this book should be addressed to Duncan Baird Publishers, at the
below address.

Created, edited, and designed by
Duncan Baird Publishers
Sixth Floor
Castle House
75–76 Wells Street
London W1T 3QH

ISBN-13: 978-1-59223-506-3
ISBN-10: 1-59223-506-9

Typeset in Palatino
Color reproduction by Colourscan, Singapore
Manufactured in Hong Kong by Imago

3 4 5 10 09 08 07 06

Editorial Consultant: Jack Tresidder
Managing Editor: Judy Barratt
Editor: Ingrid Court-Jones
Managing Designer: Manisha Patel
Designer: Simon Heard
Commissioned artwork: Helen Mills

The Amazing Memory Book is part of The Amazing Memory Kit and
must not be sold separately.

Contents

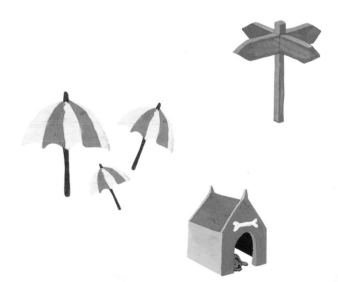

Introduction

"It's a poor sort of memory that only works backwards," the White Queen tells Alice in Lewis Carroll's *Through the Looking Glass*. The remark is surprising enough to make us laugh at its absurdity, and yet it is also, in a way, true. A good memory is one that has had a lot of "forward" (positive) training. It took me years to realize this, and to find out that I was not the slow learner I had seemed to be at school. One of my problems was that nobody had taught me how to develop my memory – I had to discover how to do this myself.

I began to gain an inkling of what my own brain could do when, at the age of 30, I tried to figure out how a man on a television show had memorized the random order of 52 playing cards in less than 3 minutes. I had no reason then to believe that I had the kind of mind that could achieve such a feat myself. On the contrary, I found it difficult to remember even familiar telephone numbers without keeping a notebook, and I thought that my poor memory was due to an inability to concentrate. Any idea that I would ever learn to memorize 2,000 digits or recall the order of 52 cards in only 35 seconds seemed fantastic. Nor did I at first realize that, in setting myself the task of solving a fairly pointless puzzle, I was embarking on an exciting and challenging path that would lead to the expansion of my whole mental horizon.

Essentially, I started to exercise my memory by using my imagination. I discovered that, by harnessing this creative ability (which is unique to humankind), I could start to develop my memory's true potential. I made up codes that replaced unmemorable things with memorable ones in the DOMINIC System (see pp.32–5), and then placed them sequentially in a familiar setting, a technique that I called the Journey Method (see pp.26–9). I soon found that such codes worked precisely because they allowed my imagination to run riot – the more crazy or bizarre they were, the more memorable they became.

It took many long hours of trial and error to hone the techniques, and I constantly adapted them until they produced the results I desired. My persistence, or perhaps I should say my stubbornness, paid off, because in 1991 I won the first World Memory Championships, an event I have continued to dominate over much of the last decade.

Some people think that I must have been born with a genius-level IQ to be able to memorize, say, the answers to 7,500 Trivial Pursuit questions after reading them through only once. Flattering as this might be, unfortunately it is not true. The fact is that these seemingly phenomenal feats can be achieved by anyone who is prepared to put time and effort into training their memory rigorously.

If you are embarrassed because you often forget people's names, if you are fed up with mislaying your house keys, or even if you wish to become the next World Memory Champion – help is at hand! In the following pages you will find all the tools you need to transform your memory. *The Amazing Memory Book* takes you step-by-step through many of the techniques that I learned, adapted, and in some cases invented, on my own voyage of memory discovery. And I share with you the systems that I have used to dominate the World Memory Championships. I hope that this book will encourage you to develop the amazing potential of your own memory.

Dominic O'Brien

How the brain stores and retrieves memories

The information we take in leaves traces or patterns of neuron activity in the brain, which form pathways. Some of this activity takes place in the short-term memory, the part that deals with immediate requirements. However, long-term memories are stored separately in the cortex – the brain's outer layer. They can reappear spontaneously if triggered by some event that restimulates a previous neuron pattern. But most recollections are responses to searches we consciously ask the brain to make.

The pathways in the brain are built up as links between neuron output fibres (axons), neuron input fibres (dendrites) and junctions (synapses). Each time we show an emotional, imaginative or intellectual interest in something, thoughts or memories are triggered. These change the physical structure of the pathways. However, when we repeat the same thought or action, we send signals along established pathways, reinforcing certain neural patterns – hence the value of repetition and revision in memory building. Equally important is the way in which we form associations between pieces of information or group them according to their type to allow our brain to locate them easily.

The brain's ability to find the information we require depends largely on how well the pathways have been established. The more links and routes that lead to a memory, the more likely we are to succeed in retrieving it.

CHAPTER ONE

LEARNING TO MEMORIZE

A good memory is a product of motivation. In early societies people were highly motivated to memorize and recall because, before writing was invented, experiences crucial to human survival had to be passed down by word of mouth. We may think that today, when we can access a vast range of information on the internet and can file data on computers, having a good memory is unnecessary. But this is not the case. Amazing as they are, computers cannot match a human memory either in selecting relevant details or in associating them quickly and intelligently with other stored information.

In this chapter we explore ways in which our memory can be improved by using the key factors of imagination, association and location, and I introduce you to two of my own techniques which have helped me become (and stay) World Memory Champion.

Mental Focus

At school I was criticized for not concentrating. My teachers implied that I could correct this simply by making more effort. If only it were that easy. An inattentive mind is the natural product of a bored brain. And information that is not coloured by personal interest nor related in intriguing ways to data already stored in the brain, sets even the keenest mind fantasizing, or reliving happy memories – in other words, day-dreaming.

The three keys to retaining interest and keeping focused are: using our imagination, understanding the things we learn, and setting ourselves goals. Bringing imagination to any subject helps to commit it to memory. You can make boring information interesting by mentally colouring it in. A strong memory also depends on our ability to link new information with data already stored in our brains, thus giving it a frame of reference in much the same way that a detective pieces together clues. Lastly, setting ourselves a goal and keeping a vivid picture of this goal in mind helps us to concentrate during the difficult, first steps of learning – for example, a piano student might imagine playing a whole concerto while practising their scales.

One of the main ways in which we assimilate information from an early age is through reading – a skill that requires good concentration. Recent research has shown that we learn more effectively if we take in information at high speed – the faster we read, the less opportunity there is for our brain to become distracted. To increase your powers of concentration, practise speed reading as often as you can. First move your finger (or some other pointer) slowly along each line and then progressively accelerate its movement until you are able to follow the text without pausing. The idea is to establish a rhythm, which will allow your brain no time for stopping or back-tracking.

Test your powers of observation

The more we notice the details about people, places and things, the more they stick in our memory. You can test and stretch your own observational skills by doing the following exercise. Choose an everyday item, such as a cup. Clear your mind and gaze at the cup for 5 minutes, noticing as much detail as you can. Start with the obvious features – its shape, colour and size – and then progress to the finer details such as pattern and texture. What kind of decoration does it have? Is its surface shiny or dull? And so on. When your 5 minutes are up, look away from the cup and try to draw it. (Your artistic ability is irrelevant here.) Label any details that you cannot sketch adequately. Then look again at the cup and compare it with your drawing. How well did you recall the details? Practise this exercise regularly to hone your powers of observation, using a variety of objects.

Memory Aids

Many people recite the rhyme "Thirty days hath September, April, June and November" to remind themselves of the number of days in each month. It works because our memory seems to enjoy and respond to "word music" just as it does to tunes or songs. Rhymes such as the one above are a form of *mnemonic* – a term coined by the ancient Greeks to describe devices that help to lodge things in the memory. Essentially, mnemonics are codes or strategies that work by linking new or abstract information with something more familiar, concrete or interesting. Groups of names, objects or numbers can thus be coded into more memorable words, phrases or sentences.

Take acronyms, in which the initial letters of a phrase or sequence of words form another word. For example, we remember NATO (which stands for North Atlantic Treaty Organization) because it is compact, it is much easier to say than the full name and it is a familiar term often used in the media. But if you wanted to remember information that was not so obviously connected – say, the names of the first three postwar US presidents – you could use the acronym TREK: TRuman, Eisenhower, Kennedy, and associate the word with marching (trekking) away from war.

Many of us will be familiar with other popular forms of mnemonics from our schooldays. For example, you might have learned how to remember the musical notes of the treble clef (EGBDF) by memorizing the line "**E**very **G**ood **B**oy **D**eserves **F**avour." Or you might have used rhymes such as: "In 1492, Columbus sailed the ocean blue," to help you recall important historical dates. Another way to remember the date 1492 would be to learn the phrase "a ship witnessed it". The trick here is that you count the number of letters in each word: 1, 4, 9, 2. This technique is quite versatile. A film buff who held separate bank accounts in Miami, Paris and Atlanta found that she never confused her PIN codes if she counted the letters in *Some Like It Hot* (4423), *Les Enfants du Paradis* (3727) and *Gone with the Wind* (4434). What is more, each film is linked with its location.

We have seen how established mnemonics, such as the rhyme about Christopher Columbus mentioned above, can be very useful, but the most effective memory aids are those that have personal meaning. Mnemonics are fun, and the time spent finding or making up your own will help to imprint them in your memory. If you need inspiration, try looking through magazines and popular newspapers, where you might come across suitable catchphrases that you can use (or adapt to personalize them) – for example "a pig in clover" (for the numbers 1326).

The Power of Visual Imagery

Nowadays there is no doubt that television, because it is a visual medium, plays an important role in improving general knowledge. Children, in particular, learn and remember a lot of information through watching TV. For example, they recall facts about animals because they see wildlife vividly portrayed in nature shows; and they memorize a great deal about foreign countries through news bulletins, which bring to life events that are far removed from their own experience. Assimilating information in this way is all very well. But how do we learn to remember facts when the images are not so

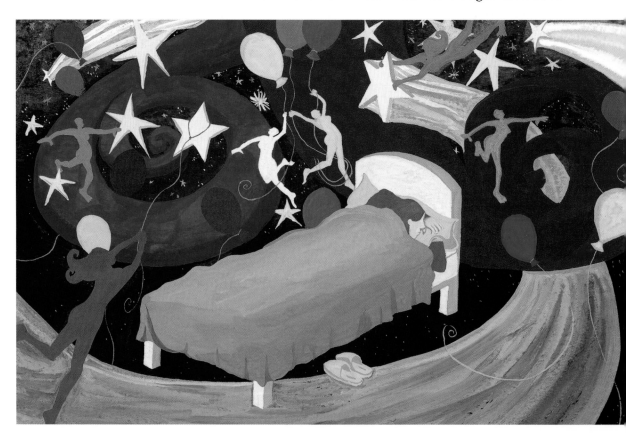

readily presented – for example, when we read a book? The answer is that we conjure up pictures in our heads – a method we employ, for example, when visualizing a character in a novel. Images are "downloaded" from our memory and we attach them to the new information as it reaches the conceptual part of the brain.

The right hemisphere of the brain, which is often called the creative side, is the seat of our imagination – the inventor of much visual imagery. The left side deals more with language, logic and calculation. Although highly artistic people sometimes neglect the left hemisphere, it is more common for people who are good at logic or figures, such as lawyers and accountants, to underestimate the role of the imaginative side of the brain. Yet this right-hand side becomes essential the moment you try to translate the mundane into the memorable. In fact, to imagine vivid mental pictures we need to use both hemispheres of the brain.

If you think that you have little imaginative ability, look at the fantastic scenarios your mind creates in dreams. They are the products of your own brain in free-wheeling play, endlessly inventing connections between disparate sensations, events, objects and people, and sending you off on bizarre adventures in which you might meet famous personalities as well as friends or acquaintances. In dreams, your brain presents dull information – say, a reminder to collect your glasses from the optician – in a dramatic form by making full use of your imagination. For example, you might dream that you go to the

theatre. When the play starts you realize that you cannot see the stage properly without your glasses, but you do not have them with you. Sitting next to you is the rock star Elton John who lends you a particularly outrageous pair of his own spectacles, but you are too embarrassed to wear them. The sheer absurdity of this dream might act as a reminder for you to collect your glasses. And with a little effort you can consciously apply the same artistic licence that makes your dreams come alive to improving your memory – making startling connections, imbuing ordinary facts with disproportionate significance and drama, and so on.

The technique of visualizing objects in a dramatic way can be applied to remembering even the most mundane data, such as everyday lists or random collections of things. Practise stretching your imagination by giving any group of objects a more theatrical context. Try remembering a selection of items that you have on your desk: a computer, a telephone, a file and a pen – at first glance, an uninspiring collection of office paraphernalia. But what if the computer were the operation control for a space shuttle; the telephone, the hot-line to the White House; the file, a classified dossier on secret agents; the pen, a miniature recording device; and so on. Suddenly the objects are exciting – and, more importantly, much more memorable.

While objects on a desk can be quite easy to remember because they belong there, it is much harder to recall unrelated events, facts, figures or faces without using your imagination to create strong associations to link them. By practising visualization as often as possible you can tone up your brain so that it learns how to attach striking images quickly to dull information, making your powers of recall both more fun and more effective.

Bringing facts alive

An active image can bring inert facts alive instantly. For example, Nobel Prize-winning physicist Richard Feynman remembered the size of a tyrannosaurus rex – 25ft (7.5 m) high with a 6-ft (2-m) wide skull – by visualizing one of these dinosaurs standing in the yard of his home, breaking an upstairs window to push its head inside. Try applying the same inventiveness to recall chemical definitions. For example, to remember that an ion is a particle carrying an electrical charge which might be positive or negative, imagine an electric **iron**. Or, to recollect the compounds that make up alcohol – carbon, hydrogen and oxygen – think of alcohol as "**C**ausing **H**ang**O**vers." You can always find a connection if you look hard enough.

Creating Links

Ever since an insurance company used the rock of Gibraltar as its logo, the advertising industry has been built on the knowledge that any name, however forgettable or commonplace it first seems, can be branded on our minds if it can be associated with something meaningful to us. The brain is able to recall a name instantly when we see a recognizable and strongly evocative image – for example, the name Hiroshima comes to mind when we see a picture of the atomic bomb's mushroom cloud. This ability also operates in everyday life when we remember, say, the name of a movie (such as *Sleepless in Seattle*) because we have visited the place mentioned in the title. These links, public or personal, are invaluable memory devices.

Linking (or association) is particularly useful for remembering groups, lists and sequences. To make maximum use of association, you need to construct a story

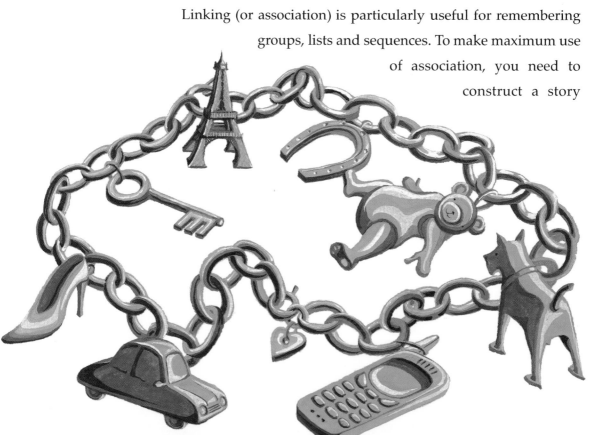

drawing not only on your memories, but also on your imagination. The more extraordinary your links are, the better a sequence will hang together in your mind. Let us return to the acronym TREK, which stands for the three postwar US presidents (see p.14). Making a word with initial letters does not work with the names of the presidents who came after Kennedy: Johnson, Nixon, Ford, Carter, Reagan, Bush (G.), Clinton, Bush (G. W.) because the initial letters do not form a memorable acronym. But you might remember a silly sequence in which Magic JOHNSON and your friend NICK'S SON tear off in a FORD CAR, chased by an alien armed with a RAY GUN. They are stopped in an amBUSH led by CLINT Eastwood, who, on seeing the alien, dives behind a BUSH.

A combination of part-names, puns and objects can also be applied in a slightly different way to memorizing a car licence plate. For example, if during a vacation in Europe a woman in a French car dented yours and drove off, you could memorize, say, 1300VX74 in a mental message such as "Unlucky! Oh, oh; Vixen! 7 days 4 repair".

When we learn history, events and their repercussions usually form powerful sequential links that help us to remember what happened in the right order. But when we have to store and recall other items in strict order – names and numbers, scientific or geographical data, meetings to attend, work to prioritize, and so on – the task becomes much harder. In this situation the technique of constructing a story, a doggerel verse, or a chain of consequences in your mind around these items can be invaluable.

Try practising your powers of association in a game with a friend. Each of you writes down a list of 20 unconnected objects and hands it to the other. Study your friend's list for 3 minutes, trying to link the words into a story. Then put the list face down, run over your story in your head and write down as many words as you can remember in the correct order. The average memory can recall 7 items, so anything higher is good; but whatever your score initially, you can improve your linking skills with practice.

Here is an example of a story that links a list of disparate words. The words are: athlete, flag, dust, goblin, temple, stone, stars, hospital, broom, gun, pot, lion, master, elevator, room, ring, newspaper, book, cross, blue. Using the list you could construct a fairly straightforward, if far-fetched story, such as: An ATHLETE who was starting to FLAG hit the DUST when a GOBLIN struck him on the TEMPLE with a STONE. This made him see STARS, so he went to HOSPITAL where, feeling strange, he seized a BROOM that he thought was a GUN and took a POTshot at an imaginary LION. The nurses managed to MASTER him and took him in the ELEVATOR to a secure ROOM where the

phone was RINGing – it was a NEWSPAPER calling to say that the goblin had been brought to BOOK and was feeling CROSS and BLUE.

Whatever the plausibility of the story, any item of information is easier to remember if it is stored in the brain as part of a chain of cause and effect, actions and consequences. There is a particularly clever nursery rhyme called "The House that Jack Built" that illustrates this point. It starts "This is the house that Jack built. This is the malt that lay in the house that Jack built," and so on, building up to the final part which reveals a whole long sequence of consequences:

This is the farmer sowing his corn
that kept the cock that crowed in the morn
that woke the priest all shaven and shorn
that married the man all tattered and torn
that kissed the maiden all forlorn
that milked the cow with the crumpled horn
that tossed the dog
that worried the cat
that killed the rat
that ate the malt
that lay in the house that Jack built.

Here, the structure of rhyme and rhythm – and the chain of consequences – is so strong that the verse is remarkably easy to remember and recite both backward or forward.

Places in the Mind

How is it that we often see a familiar face but cannot "place" it? For example, a contestant in a television quiz show may be someone whose face we recognize, but we do not immediately remember that he is the man who works behind the meat counter in our local supermarket. The difficulty is not so much that he is wearing a black silk shirt instead of the white apron we normally see him in, but that he is completely out of context.

A sense of place is fundamental to how we store and retrieve items in our memory. How might you remember what your partner wore the first time you were introduced to him or her? Probably you would cast your mind back to the place where you met, and, as you

Building a memory chest

Imagine you are asked to name the 13 countries of South America in decreasing order of size (Brazil, Argentina, Peru, Colombia, Bolivia, Venezuela, Chile, Paraguay, Ecuador, Uruguay, Guyana, Surinam, French Guiana). To help you memorize them, try constructing an imaginary chest with a drawer for each country, the biggest at top left, the smallest at bottom right. Place objects or letters in each drawer to help trigger the name of the country when you open the drawer. For example: you could put a PARAchutist in the PARAguay drawer, some BOLlinger champagne in the BOLivia drawer and so on, until each country is represented. To remember all the countries you simply open each drawer mentally, in order, from top left to bottom right.

build up the details, so your partner's blue sweater, red dress or whatever they were wearing, would come back to you.

Using context of place as a mnemonic aid dates back to the ancient Greeks' who are believed to have been the first to develop the principle of "locus". They assembled in their minds the items they wanted to remember and mentally ordered them against a familiar background, such as a public square, placing one item next to a statue, another beside a fountain, and so on. In this way, the Greeks were able to bring a coherence to an otherwise random set of objects, points in a speech or items on a list. Then, by mentally retracing their steps through the square, they could bring each item back to mind.

Therefore one effective way to remember things and fix them in a definite order is to mentally peg them against a background that you can readily visualize and on which you can organize them in sequence. The route could range from a tour of the pictures or ornaments in your house, from top to bottom, to a walk around your local park, using the pond, playground and other features as your stages.

Walking through Memories

We come now to the technique that I have developed to fix long sequences of points or lists of items in the mind – I call it the Journey Method. It combines the three key techniques of location (place), association (links) and imagination, and exploits one of the most ancient of human skills – the capacity to remember features of a familiar landscape, no matter how barren. Certain peoples, such as the Australian Aboriginals or the San of the Kalahari Desert region, are renowned for their ability to orient themselves in an apparently

featureless environment by, for example, using the clues provided by a bent tree or slight slope in the terrain.

If we are asked to recount a route that we frequently take, most of us can provide a pretty accurate description, and we do this by retracing the route in our mind. In a city we can often recall every small short-cut on the way to work. In the same way, jump-jockeys can remember every fence on a racecourse, and skiers every tight turn or speed bump on a descent of several miles. Any familiar route with enough memorable features can be used as a mental pathway along which you can store items you wish to remember in a fixed order.

It is only by using a strategem such as the Journey Method that memory champions can recall astonishingly long sequences of items. I once memorized a sequence of 2,080 cards displayed randomly for just a few seconds each. How did I do it? As I knew there were going to be 40 packs of cards with 52 cards in each, I made sure that I could mentally retrace my steps along 40 familiar routes, each with 52 recognizable stops at which I could place characters invented for each card. It took me 8 hours to memorize the cards and 2 hours to recite them back as I travelled along each journey in turn.

Few people want to spend months training for memory marathons like this. But applied to less daunting tasks, the Journey Method is both practical and effective. All you need to do is fix a number of routes in your mind, establish memorable points along them and create a sharp image of each item you wish to remember at each stop. Success depends on how much imagination you use to associate the items and stops.

Unless an item or name suggests an immediate connection with the place where you are putting it, you need to introduce an imaginative link that joins the two elements. Use the kind of wordplay you employed to build your memory chest (see box, p.24), putting as much dramatic impact into each scene as you can. Let us say you choose your route to work as a way to remember Shakespeare's 10 tragedies in the order he is thought to have written them. The stages you decide to use are: your neighbour's gate, the house opposite yours, the park, the delicatessen, the bank, the sports centre, the movie theatre, the bus stop, the travel agency and the supermarket.

Stepping outside, you meet your neighbour at his gate. He is doing pirouettes and wearing ballet tights (*Titus Andronicus*). You cross the street and notice the local gallant outside the house opposite, serenading a girl (*Romeo and Juliet*). You walk up the street and come to the park, where you are amazed to see an alien balancing two huge jewels on a seesaw (*Julius Caesar*). Passing the delicatessen you feel ravenous when you see a leg of ham hanging in the window (*Hamlet*). Next, outside the bank,

The starry highway

Each of the 12 signs of the Zodiac has its own symbols with which it has been associated since ancient times. We can use these symbols as aids to help us remember the star signs in a specific order. Practise and test your ability to construct a memory journey by dropping the 12 Zodiac signs along a familiar route that has 12 stages.

The order of the Zodiac signs is: Aries (ram), Taurus (bull), Gemini (twins), Cancer (crab), Leo (lion), Virgo (virgin), Libra (scales), Scorpio (scorpion), Sagittarius (archer), Capricorn (sea-goat), Aquarius (water carrier), Pisces (fish). Following this sequence, place a sign at each consecutive stage of your journey, using an imaginative association to link the conventional symbol with the relevant stage.

you listen to a North African busker playing a cello (*Othello*). Then, in front of the sports centre, you are surprised to find a huge clock on the sidewalk (*Timon of Athens*). By the movie theatre you see some youths leering (*King Lear*) at a pretty girl standing at the bus stop – she is wearing a Scottish tartan skirt (*Macbeth*). In the window of the travel agency you watch a man charming a snake out of a basket (*Antony and Cleopatra*). And finally, just before you reach the office, you pass a supermarket which has a special offer on coriander (*Coriolanus*).

The Number–Shape System

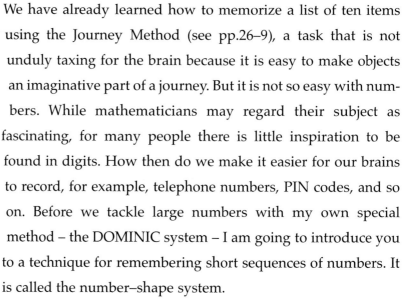

We have already learned how to memorize a list of ten items using the Journey Method (see pp.26–9), a task that is not unduly taxing for the brain because it is easy to make objects an imaginative part of a journey. But it is not so easy with numbers. While mathematicians may regard their subject as fascinating, for many people there is little inspiration to be found in digits. How then do we make it easier for our brains to record, for example, telephone numbers, PIN codes, and so on. Before we tackle large numbers with my own special method – the DOMINIC system – I am going to introduce you to a technique for remembering short sequences of numbers. It is called the number–shape system.

Each number from 0 to 9 is instantly recognizable by its written shape. If we choose an everyday item that has a similar shape to a particular number, the digit ceases to be a bland cipher and instead becomes an object. For example, 2 is reminiscent of a swan. So every time we wish to memorize a 2, we think of a beautiful swan. You may wish to think up your own number–shape images or you can use the established associations, which are as follows: 0 is represented as a ball, a hoop or a ring; 1 is a candle, a pencil or a telegraph pole; 2, a swan or a snake; 3, a pair of handcuffs or lips in profile; 4, the sail of a boat or a flag; 5, a hook or a seahorse; 6, an elephant's trunk, a metal detector or a golf club; 7, a boomerang or a shark's fin; 8, an hour-glass or a snowman; and 9, a balloon on a string, or a monocle.

When you have familiarized yourself with the number–shapes, try using them to help you remember a variety of data. For example, if you need to remember that there are seven deadly sins, you might conjure up an image of the devil throwing a boomerang; or if you wish to memorize the 4-digit alarm code for your house – 8643 – you might envisage an hour-glass on your gatepost (8), an elephant tethered at your gate (6), a flag (4) hanging above your porch, and a policeman holding a pair of handcuffs (3) by the front door. Here, as with the Journey Method, the three keys are working together as a team. Your imagination makes associations between the numbers and the location – your house. As with the other techniques we have considered, the number–shape system works best if you make your images as vivid and interesting as possible.

The DOMINIC System

Like many people, I used to have difficulty remembering a list of digits – even a phone number – and I hankered after finding a way to make abstract numbers more tangible or memorable. The system I created for this purpose uses the acronym DOMINIC – Decipherment of Mnemonically Interpreted Numbers Into Characters.

We have already seen that an easy way to recall short groups of digits – PIN codes and so on – is to concoct a sentence in which each word has the number of letters denoted by each digit of the code (see p.15) or to use the number–shape system (see pp.30–31). But to memorize larger numbers of, say, 10 digits or more, or tables of figures, a more creative mental abacus is necessary. I decided to turn figures into personalities by thinking of them first as letters, then as the initials of people's names. I eventually came up with a 10-letter alphabet in which each letter stands for a digit from 0 to 9. By putting a 0 before each single digit – 00, 01, and so on – I made every number between 0 and 99 form a pair. When I converted the pairs into letters, I had a series of initials, which represented names I could remember vividly because they belonged either to famous people or to friends or acquaintances.

The most obvious number–letter system is A to I for 1 to 9, but I found that I associated some numbers more readily with other letters. So, the letters I use in my own number–letter code are A, B, C, D, E (as 1–5), together with the letter O standing for 0. Then, S for 6 (because of the "s" sound), G for 7 (after the

G7 group of economic powers), H for 8 (because it is the eighth letter of the alphabet), and N for 9 (again because of the sound). With these 10 associations, I was able to turn the figures from 0 to 99 into a hundred characters. I then realized that, with long sequences of numbers, there was no need to add initial zeroes because the digits could be paired off. For example, you could translate 236322287217 (12 digits) into the six pairs of initials BC (23), SC (63), BB (22), BH (28), GB (72), AG (17). Let us say these initials suggested Bill Clinton, Sean Connery, Benjamin Britten, Bob Hoskins, George Bush, Al Gore. You could then fix the number in your mind by creating a sequential visualization around Bill Clinton inviting Sean Connery to bring Benjamin Britten and Bob Hoskins to a reception organized for George Bush by Al Gore. The unlikelihood of Gore organizing a reception for Bush would make such a mnemonic device all the more memorable.

A good way to practise the DOMINIC system is to memorize a list of dates. Say that you wish to remember the birthdays of six relatives: Sam,

Penny, Helen, Tom, Mary and Rob. Arranging the dates by days then months, their birthdays fall on 13/02, 18/06, 26/08, 22/10, 28/11 and 15/12. You translate these figures into the initial letters that identify people in your personality list: AC/OB (Anton Chekhov and Otto von Bismarck), AH/OS (Alfred Hitchcock and Omar Sharif), BS/OH (Bram Stoker and Oliver Hardy), BB/AO (Brigitte Bardot and Aristotle Onassis), BH/AA (Bob Hope and André Agassi), AE/AB (Albert Einstein and Alexander Bell).

Then, to memorize each relative's birthday, imagine a scene taking place in- or outside their house. For example, visualizing your uncle Sam's house, picture Anton Chekhov towing a battleship, which is Otto von Bismarck's associated prop, up the drive. (Notice that here we combine the first personality with the second personality's prop.) Next you take a trip to your cousin Penny's house, where you head for the shower room to freshen up, only to find Alfred Hitchcock playing a game of bridge (Omar Sharif's favourite pastime) there. Over at your aunt Helen's house, you find Bram Stoker, dressed as Dracula, in the master bedroom acting the fool – Oliver Hardy's profession. At cousin Tom's house you see Brigitte Bardot sunning herself on a yacht in the garden (the yacht, of course, is associated with Aristotle Onassis). Over to great-aunt Mary's house now where you find Bob Hope playing tennis (André Agassi's profession) in the entrance hall. And finally, at cousin Rob's apartment there is Albert Einstein on a cell 'phone (Alexander Bell invented the telephone) discussing the finer points of a brilliant new equation.

A frequent, quick review of these locations will ensure that you never forget your relatives' birthdays again.

Quick calculation

Try this party trick using the DOMINIC system. Ask a friend to write down and read out to you 4 columns of 10 single digits, as in the example below. You are going to give your friend a grand total – the sum of the 10 rows:

```
7 8 6 1
8 3 5 4
5 6 1 7
9 5 4 0
9 1 3 8
3 4 8 5
5 2 1 4
4 0 2 6
8 3 3 2
8 1 2 5
```
66 33 35 42

7,861+8,354+5,617, and so on. Mentally add each *column* as its digits are read out. Next, convert the total, which will consist of 2 digits, into a pair of initials and put a personality in its place. Do this with each column's total. Then imagine the 4 personalities in a football stadium, each sitting a seat lower than the one before and further to the right, like this:

Stephen Spielberg	66
Charlie Chaplin	33
Clint Eastwood	35
David Bowie	42
Grand total	69,692

To recall the 4 totals, just remember the 4 personalities. By recalling them in the position shown above, you can produce the grand total by adding up the 4 totals from left to right. You will appear to be a genius!

CHAPTER TWO

PUTTING MEMORY INTO ACTION

Memory techniques of any kind are effective only if you put them into practice regularly on the "use it or lose it" principle. Understanding the Journey Method or the DOMINIC system is not enough. The systems will not work for you unless you work on them. For example, with the DOMINIC system you need to memorize the number–alphabet and then practise by applying it to as many numbers as possible until you can code and decode figures with consummate ease.

Once you have mastered these systems, you are ready to put your memory techniques into action. In this chapter, we learn how to remember names and faces and how to apply the Journey Method in particular situations, such as public speaking, interviews and meetings. We also explore how to memorize a whole deck of cards using the DOMINIC system, and how to remember trivia so that we can become a "quiz whizz".

Matching Names to Faces

We see millions of faces in a lifetime, but usually we can instantly recognize one that means something to us, whether we see the person from the front or in profile, and whether they are laughing, crying or sneezing.

Putting a name to a face is not so easy, but this is not surprising. Our encounters with most people are so fleeting that the brain does not store their images in our long-term memory, which makes it difficult for us to remember someone we meet in passing.

The experience of meeting a number of people at once and then forgetting their names is common to all of us. But by practising the techniques of association described below, I found that I was able to memorize the names of more than a hundred complete strangers in the space of 20 minutes.

When we are introduced to a group of people, we are often distracted – it is noisy; there is too much going on around us; or perhaps we are feeling self-conscious. Whatever the reason, we do not concentrate properly. So the first step in such a situation is to relax, slow down and pay careful attention to each person's face. It may also help to repeat at least their first name – you could say something like "Good to meet you, Mary," before passing on to the next person. After the introductions have been completed, mentally run through all the names and faces again and do not be afraid to check any you had difficulty with – nobody minds being asked to repeat their name.

As you meet somebody new, ask yourself three questions. What is my first impression of this person? Is there any obvious link between their name and their face? Can I associate either with a place I know? The aim is to light up the person in your mind by associating their name with their face, and then to peg this link to a familiar backdrop. You could call this process LAMP – Likeness, Association, My Place.

Let us say that you meet a jolly person called Mary Leake, who has a long chin. She does not remind you of anyone (the swiftest way to characterize a face), but you can link her cheerful demeanour with her name by thinking of a leek with a happy face (merry leek). Mary has a long chin, which sounds like "long gin", so you imagine her drinking a gin and tonic in your favourite bar. You have now supplied a context that adds visual and sensory impact to her image in your mind. The fact that she turns out to be less merry than you first thought makes the image no less effective. The important thing is that, by forging the associations and placing her in a personal context, you have made her memorable.

A less distinctive face or a more unusual name might be

harder to pin down, but if you practise you will quickly increase your ability to make associations. Remember that names do not have to sound exactly like the things you associate with them for memory to be triggered. Say you have difficulty remembering actress Kim Basinger's name. In order to memorize it you picture her in a role from one of her films – a singer in a dim bar. "Dim bar singer" sounds enough like "Kim Basinger" to bring her name instantly to mind whenever you recall the associated image.

While rushed introductions to large groups of people can be unavoidable – for example, at parties – in many other situations, such as small meetings, you have time to study a face and discover more about a person than just their name. Finding out their occupation can add another dimension to the associations you make, and also help you to recall impressive facts about people whom you have met only once. For example, if Mary Leake told you that she was a manicurist you could imagine elaborate nails on the fingers holding her glass. But remember, the key links to establish are between face and name and some element of either that links them to a familiar place.

Testing your skills of association

Use word-play to link each of the 10 people named below with the first impressions they make, so that a memorable image of each person performing an action emerges. Try breaking the names, and the descriptions into smaller words. For example, Belle Mascal is described as "ample", which can be broken up into "a.m. pull". It is then easy to see Belle Mascal as a large woman ringing the bells for early morning mass (mass-call). When you have created all 10 images, cover the left column and see if you can recall each person's name accurately. Next, place all your characters along a 10-stage journey, linking each person to a stage. Then try to recall the names and attributes in the order in which they have been placed along the journey.

Name	First Impression
Belle Mascal	Ample
Nigel Marriner	Pop-eyed
Sally Little	Grumpy
David Porter	Sheepish
Tina Holcroft	Mousy
Charles Bolde	Hawk-nosed
Dorothy Taylor	Dowdy
Egon Phillips	Self-satisfied
Trixie Gaysford	Has laughter wrinkles
Harry Lovelock	Has spiky hair

Walking the Talk

Most practised public speakers carry notes of their speech with them, usually summarized in key points on flash cards headed by sequential trigger-words that fluently link one train of thought to the next. By referring to these cards, speakers lessen the risk of losing their train of thought or leaving something out. It is better still to make the notes and memorize them so well that you can leave the flash cards in your pocket. The Journey Method, which we learned about on pp.26–9, will enable you do this with confidence because you can simply "walk" through your talk.

Speech-making is all about preparation. Begin by planning your speech well in advance of your delivery date. Write down the key points you wish to make and then make a rough draft. Go through the draft, dropping anything that you decide does not work and adding amendments to make it livelier. Then "polish" your speech until you are completely happy with it. Start committing the speech to memory by reading it through silently at least twice. Then rehearse it several times out loud, referring to the "script" as little as possible. When you have finished delivering it from memory, look back at the written version. Flag any points at which you lost your way or left material out.

Next, summarize your speech in about 10 short notes, each headed by a "trigger" word, which will instantly bring to mind the relevant part of your speech. Make the images especially strong for the sections that you had difficulty recalling during your practice. Then choose a journey or route that you have already used for memory work and mentally walk it, depositing your 10 trigger images at 10 stages along the way.

Finally, mentally retrace your route once on each of the five days before you give your speech. (It is a golden rule of memory that revising something five times embeds it in the mind.) As you travel the route in your mind recite your speech using the 10 images that you have placed there as triggers. You should now have the whole speech safely stored. What is more, it is stored along a journey you have often made already. This should give you all the confidence you need to stand up and speak fluently. If you seem to be speaking effortlessly, the audience will relax – and so will you.

Poems by Heart

A good poem captures its subject matter and the mood of the poet with an economy of words. And the language of poetry is full of evocative imagery that appeals directly to our imagination – which is why reading and memorizing verse is an excellent way to improve memory skills.

The brain also responds instinctively to rhyme and rhythm because these form a coherent pattern. In many modern poems, the pattern may be subtle and you need to search for it. Take the poem opposite, *The Wild Swans at Coole* by W. B. Yeats. The poet's uncanny ear for "word music" enables him to use broken metres that flow past line endings to form a steadily beating pattern of stresses. Each verse has three pairs of lines. In the first two pairs in each verse, there are seven stresses (4+3). But the last pair of lines in each verse has eight stresses, with a full rhyme on the fifth and eighth stresses (in all but the first stanza, which has a near-rhyme). Read the poem aloud until you have found these patterns – the first step to memorizing it.

Next, remembering the three golden keys to memory – imagination, association and location – reduce each line (or pair of lines) to a key image and place it at a stage on a familiar journey. For example, for the first line: "The trees are in their autumn beauty," you might see a beautiful woman sitting in a tree, leaves falling all around her. Put this image at the first stage of the journey. Continue to use the Journey Method (see pp.26–9) with the rest of the lines and see if you can memorize the whole poem in about 30 minutes.

The Wild Swans at Coole

The trees are in their autumn
* beauty,*
The woodland paths are dry,
Under the October twilight the water
Mirrors a still sky;
Upon the brimming water among
* the stones*
Are nine-and-fifty swans.

The nineteenth autumn has come
* upon me*
Since I first made my count;
I saw, before I had well finished,
All suddenly mount
And scatter wheeling in great
* broken rings*
Upon their clamorous wings.

I have looked upon those
* brilliant creatures*
And now my heart is sore.
All's changed since I, hearing

* at twilight,*
The first time on this shore,
The bell-beat of their wings above
* my head,*
Trod with a lighter tread.

Unwearied still, lover by lover,
They paddle in the cold
Companionable streams or climb
* the air;*
Their hearts have not grown old;
Passion or conquest, wander where
* they will,*
Attend upon them still.

But now they rest on the still water,
Mysterious, beautiful;
Among what rushes will they build,
By what lake's edge or pool
Delight men's eyes when I awake
* some day*
To find they have flown away?

Interviews and Meetings

Preparation is just as important for an interview as it is for a speech. The interview may start with your potential boss asking questions about you that you can easily answer. But he or she will soon move on to probe why the post and the organization interest you. This is your chance to clinch the job by showing that you have done your research and are knowledgeable about the vacancy. Referring to notes would give a poor impression of your confidence.

Find out as much as you can about the company and the job well before the interview. Then write down in order of priority

what you wish to say and what questions you can ask to show your interest. Reduce this list to a series of, say, 12 key points around which you can form strong mental images. Then choose one of the familiar routes that you have already used for memory work. Finally, place your images at 12 stages along the journey, ensuring that you make powerful connections between the stages and the images.

Committing such a list to memory will help you to relax in what is nearly always a stressful situation. Remember that the ability to relax itself creates a good impression. If you are interrupted, take a moment to fix in your mind the journey stage you have reached – you can then return to it, and carry on. The same applies if the interviewer prematurely brings up one of the points that you have allocated to a later stage. Simply return to where you left off and, when you come to it, miss out the stage that has already been addressed.

Try a similar technique at meetings. Prepare your contribution to the discussion by making a list of key points and mentally link them with stages along a journey. This will enable you to recall your points and make them appear logical and well-thought-out. You will also demonstrate your command of the situation by showing that you can speak without notes.

If, while someone is speaking, you wish to memorize certain issues so that you can raise them later in the meeting, place the points mentally along another, shorter, route. Then, when it is your turn to comment, you will be able to recall them in the order in which they were discussed and make a further effective contribution.

Calling the Cards

Memorizing a randomly-dealt deck of cards at speed is one of the best tests of your ability to use a combination of both the DOMINIC system and the Journey Method. Committing a sequence of 52 cards to memory might seem a mind-boggling task, but it becomes altogether easier if you first convert the whole pack into 52 highly individual and memorable characters.

Begin with the cards from ace to 10 and convert them to the 10-letter alphabetical code as set out in the DOMINIC system (see pp.32–5). Use A for an ace, B for a 2, C for a 3, D for a 4, E for a 5, S for a 6, G for a 7, H for an 8, N for a 9 and O – the letter allocated to 0 in the DOMINIC System – for 10. Then pair each letter with C, D, H and S (clubs, diamonds, hearts and spades). In other words, the ace of hearts becomes AH, the six of spades SS, the 10 of diamonds OD, and so on. This gives you pairs of initials that you can associate with the names of familiar or famous people.

Next, choose names for the court cards – the jacks, queens and kings, making sure that they do not duplicate any that you have already assigned to the lower cards. You might have Princess Diana as the queen of hearts, Madonna as the queen of clubs, Liz Taylor as the queen of diamonds and the best woman gardener you know as the queen of spades. Add four senior men (such as Clark Gable as king of hearts), four young men (perhaps Keanu Reeves as jack of clubs?), and you have a full deck of characters.

You now need to practise memorizing the whole deck by repeatedly dealing and naming a few cards at a time, then gradually increasing the number of cards you memorize. When you are thoroughly familiar with the pack, you should recognize a card not as the three of clubs, but as, say, Cindy Crawford. To remember cards in sequence, you then need to choose a journey along which to place your characters.

Although we have used memory journeys throughout the book, so far we have not needed as many stages as 52. While it would be perfectly feasible to think of a journey with 52 stages, it might be easier to use four shorter journeys, each with 13 stages. Let us say that you belong to a health club and work out there following a regular routine. Your 13 areas could be the entrance lobby, reception desk, locker room, warm-up gym area, mezzanine floor with exercise bikes, step machine, jogging belt, rowing machine,

weights section, swimming pool, steam room, showers, juice bar.

Once such a sequence of stages is fixed in your mind, you can watch the fall of 13 cards and see, for example, Cindy Crawford (3 of clubs) filming her new exercise video in the the lobby as you come in; Geena Davis (7 of diamonds) swatting flies at the reception desk; Sean Connery (6 of clubs) dressing himself in a dinner suit in the locker room; Saddam Hussein (6 of hearts) setting fire to the warm-up mats; Audrey Hepburn (ace of hearts) hitching up her nun's habit on the exercise bike next to you, and so on. These encounters are all likely to look startling in the familiar context of your health club and therefore they will be memorable.

When the first 13 cards have been dealt and memorized, you move on to your next location – perhaps the zoo to which you sometimes take your child and where you know the exact sequence of enclosures along a visiting circuit. Here, the next 13 card personalities interact with vividly different animals. For example, you might find an elephant stealing Arnold Schwarzenegger's (ace of spades) suitcase; or a group of gorillas completely captivated by Celine Dion's (three of

Total recall

On January 26, 2001 I appeared on the *Guinness World of Records* TV show in Munich, Germany, where I set a new world record for the simultaneous memorization of two decks of playing cards.

First, each deck of 52 cards was shuffled. Next, each deck was placed separately face down in front of me. Then I memorized two cards at a time by dealing one card from one deck (with my left hand) and one from the other (with my right hand). It took me about 3½ minutes to commit all 104 cards to memory. I was then able to recall all of one deck, followed by all of the other deck, with no errors.

diamonds) singing; or Charlton Heston (three of hearts) hurtling around a paddock in his chariot with two irate rhinoceroses in hot pursuit; and so on. When you have memorized cards 14 to 26, move on to the third journey (cards 27 to 39), and finally the fourth journey (cards 40 to 52), until you have memorized the whole deck.

Now, just sit back, relax, and allow all the imaginative images to come back to you one by one, as you rerun the "movie" of each of your amazing journeys in your head. Then, discover how successful your memorizations were by going through the deck again and converting the personalities, one by one, back into cards.

The Trivia Wizard

Even when we memorize sequences of cards or other data that we wish to recall only once, the information is stored in our long-term memory, and it often takes us a while to forget these items. This is why I have built up a stock of many different journeys along which I can store data. However, we need to take a different approach if we wish to memorize general knowledge to recall in quizzes and games such as Trivial Pursuit, where questions flip from one field of general knowledge to another and the answers have to be found rapidly.

The way to do this is to use a technique similar to the one employed when remembering names and faces (see pp.38–41), by creating an image that sets each fact in an associated mental backdrop. Then you need to revise what you have stored, not once but regularly. I have memorized thousands of Trivial Pursuit questions and answers in this way and can retrieve them almost instantly. They pop out because I have built in a trigger mechanism between the question and the answer. Here are some examples. What is the name for a young pigeon? Answer: a squab – I see pigeons SQUABbling for crumbs on my window ledge. What do psychiatrists call fear of crowds? Answer: demophobia – I see a mob DEMOnstrating in Palestine. What is the collective name for a group of mules? Answer: a span – I see a line of baggage mules on a swaying rope bridge SPANning a ravine in Mexico. What is the name of Toronto's main airport? Answer: Pearson – I see a girl standing on an airport runway in TORrential rain, washing her face with PEAR'S soap.

You can expand your general knowledge by turning facts gleaned from newspapers and magazines into quiz-type questions and answers. Remember the golden rule: if you review information five times, you will be able to recall it for life. I suggest that you revise your question-and-answer associations a day or two after memorizing them and run through them again every few months. You may find yourself becoming a veritable "quiz whizz"!

Which Muse?

Foreign names often have to be broken up before you can see question–answer linkages in a quiz. Asked which art Terpsichore (Greek muse of dancing) protected, you might remember that rehearsing ballet is no "chore" for a "tipsy" dancer. Practise by trying to find memory links for the other eight Muses. They are: Calliope (epic poetry), Clio (history), Erato (love poetry), Euterpe (music), Melpomene (tragedy), Polyhymnia (singing), Thalia (comedy and pastoral poetry), Urania (astronomy).

CHAPTER THREE

USING THE AMAZING MEMORY KIT

Giving your mind a regular workout can be as enjoyable as practising your golf swing – and is probably a lot more fun than lifting weights. The most wonderful thing about exercising your memory is that it is just like playing a game – and the more fun the game, the more effective your mental workout.

So far we have talked about boosting your memory power to remember lists, birthdays and PIN codes, decks of cards and general knowledge. In this chapter we take a look at how to use all the special elements of the Amazing Memory Kit – the Memory Journey Maps and the Memory Deck – to help you to develop your imaginative powers and stretch your memory to the full. Practise as often as you can, testing yourself not only against your own previous attempts, but also against friends and family who have no knowledge of the techniques that you have learned in this book. Use the components of the box to monitor how your memory develops. The most amazing memory journey of all starts here!

The Journey Maps and the Deck

The **Memory Journey Maps** and the **Memory Deck** are designed to work hand in hand. The former comprise four journeys: *From the Countryside to the Shore*; *Around the Garden*; *Around the Town*; and *Around the Department Store*. Each journey has 25 distinct landmarks or stages (these are listed on the following pages) on which you can position 25 items that you want to remember. Each Memory Map concertina depicts two journeys – one on each side. Switch journeys simply by turning the Journey Maps over. You can stretch your abilities by working with more than one journey. As you become proficient, you can run one journey into another (in any order) so that, as soon as you are able to memorize 25 objects on one journey, you can progress to memorizing 50, 75 and ultimately 100 items by using two, three or all four journeys. To give you a ready-made supply of items to remember, the Memory Deck consists of 100 double-sided cards. On one side are pictures of everyday items; on the other, the numbers from one to 100. The numbers and the images are not intended to be used at the same time – in other words you use either the images (to help you exercise your ability to remember lists) or the numbers (to help train you to remember dates and other numbers, and to use the DOMINIC system) at any one time.

So how does it work? Taking the journey From the Countryside to the Shore as an example, you decide whether you wish to memorize numbers or objects. Say you choose objects. You count off 25 cards from the top of the Memory Deck to obtain 25 items to be memorized. You shuffle the cards and stack them on a table, numbers uppermost (so that the objects are obscured). Open the journey out in front of you. Turning up the first card, match that object (for example, the catapult) to the first stage of the journey (the farmhouse), using your imagination to create a link between the two. Perhaps the farmer is standing on the roof of the farmhouse catapulting horse manure at you! You then turn up the second card and link it to the second stage, and so on, until you have memorized all 25 items. When you are working your way through the cards, be careful to place them back in a new pile, face down, in the same order – you will need to refer back to them to check your memorization. When you have finished memorizing the cards, look back at the journey. Beginning at the first

landmark, and working around the path in order, recall all the items that you placed along the route. Note them down on a piece of paper as you bring them back to mind, one by one. When you have remembered all 25 items, check your written list against the cards.

When memorizing numbers, use the DOMINIC system (see pp.32–5) to convert numbers into personalities (remembering first to add a zero in front of single digits) and then link the personalities imaginatively with a stage along the route.

Aim to learn the routes of the Journey Maps by heart so that you don't have to refer back to the Maps themselves when recalling items or numbers. Instead, mentally walk the route, and do the whole thing entirely from your amazing memory! Eventually, devise journeys of your own.

Listed opposite, are each of the 25 stages in the four Map journeys.

- From the Countryside to the Shore: farmhouse; barn; windmill; scarecrow; hay; signpost; pigsty; bench; fallen tree; beehives; lake; bridge; beach bar; lifeguard post; umbrellas; safety flag; showers; surf hut; hammock; beach huts; volleyball court; lifesaving ring; pier; ice cream hut; lighthouse.
- Around the Garden: greenhouse; vegetable garden; compost heap; chicken coop; sandpit; tree house; play house; swing; swimming pool; shed; climbing frame; sunflower bed; lamp post; fountain; trellis; barbecue; rose bush; sundial; maze; statue; dog kennel; bird table; apple tree; weather vane; gate.
- Around the Town: traffic light; news stand; fire hydrant; apartment blocks; church; hospital; obelisk; flower stand; municipal building; public lavatories; police station; factory; school; fruit stand; taxi stand; diner; ice rink; public telephones; fire station; train station; parking lot; trash can; bus stop; stop sign.
- Around the Department Store: entrance; shoes; notions (haberdashery); lingerie; hats; make-up; jewelry; bridalwear; ladies' wear; children's wear; men's wear; toys; sports; furniture; bathrooms; paint; lighting; kitchens; computers; electrical goods; gardening; juice bar; glassware; books; checkout.

Conclusion: The Magic of Memory

A good memory gives us confidence – the confidence to know that we will remember the people we meet; the confidence to be able to call upon information or arguments when we need them (formally, as when preparing a speech or an interview, or informally, in a quiz game); and the confidence to be able to recall telephone numbers or important dates without having to refer to an address book or diary. The fundamental message of this book is that, if you learn the techniques and practise the exercises I have shown you, you will not only develop an amazing memory, but also benefit from the greater self-confidence that having this skill brings. In addition, by honing our powers of imagination and association through memory training techniques, we learn to appreciate the world more keenly (because our imagination depends on what our senses take in). Moreover, we encourage our brain to work more efficiently at linking the many pieces of information it is fed in a single minute, let alone in an hour or a day!

Memory champions are sometimes regarded as tricksters or magicians. But all they are doing is tapping into the magic of a well-trained memory. With a little effort, you can develop this power yourself. If the techniques I have mentioned in this book can be described as the "language" for memorization, you yourself must invent the vocabulary – with memory images drawn from your own environment and interests.

It takes time to develop an easy familiarity with your bank of images, associations, locations and journeys, so do not expect too much too soon. Pace yourself sensibly – the brain, like the body, can become fatigued and need rest. That is why students who have a good night's sleep before an exam perform better than those who have stayed up all night cramming facts into their heads.

Training your memory is an on-going process. Keep revising and repeating what you have learned and never imagine that you have progressed too far to go back over the basics now and then – just as the exterior of a house needs repainting every few years to ensure that it withstands all weathers, so the building blocks of your memory need regular care and attention. Refreshing the memory is especially important as we get older, as it halts the natural tendency of the brain's neuron signals to weaken.

Despite great advances in technology, computers are no match for the wonderful human brain. And as more becomes known about how our memory works, it is likely that today's memory feats will be far surpassed. I hope this book will have put into your hands techniques that will show you the power of your own amazing memory – even better, I hope to meet you at a future World Memory Championship.

Good luck!